GW00870085

Hugh and the Manatee

By Dr. Mary Helen Hensley

Illustrated

By Max Gordon

Cover Illustrator: Max Gordon

ISBN: 978-1-8381691-6-9

www.bookhubpublishing.com

(091) 846953 (087) 2246885
Twitter: @bookhubpublish
Instagram: bookhub_publishing
For further information re international distribution contact
info@bookhubpublishing.com

Dr. Mary Helen Hensley may be booked to speak or present on the
themes of the book by contacting Susan McKenna at
www.bookhubpublishing.com
or (091) 846953.

Book Hub Publishing and the Author are committed to inclusion
and diversity.

On a beautiful Spring day in May of 2019, I was with my family at DeLeon Springs in Volusia County, Florida, celebrating my mother's ninetieth birthday. The Sugar Mill restaurant has been a favorite spot of mine since I was a child. It sits on the edge of the gorgeous springs where, just a few miles away, I saw my very first manatee when I was three years old. I was in awe of this curious creature and nearly fifty years later, those same magical waters inspired the setting for a book I had been wanting to write for quite some time.

My nephew, Max, a graphic artist living in NYC, was also eating 'make your own' pancakes with us that morning, around the griddles situated in the center of the restaurant's tables. As we poured the batter and made shapes and faces that we then garnished with blueberries, strawberries and all sorts of delicious toppings, I told Max that I really wanted to write a series of books for pre-teens that broke through the stereotypical gender identity roles typically found in children's literature.

I shared with him that I wanted to create stories in which *every* child could find themselves. I had a rough idea of how the first story would unfold, but on that day, while eating pancakes and looking out at the magical springs, Hugh and the Manatee was born. I didn't have to say another word. Max fully supported my dream and its mission and agreed to help me bring Hugh to life.

We are thrilled to share the first book in this series. Our hope is that its message will touch the hearts of our adult LGBTQ friends who never had the chance to read about a child that looked or felt like they did. For our younger readers, we want to offer a broader perspective, a new dialogue and a better understanding of what the *real world,* and ALL of its people, actually looks like. Throughout this series, we will strive to support our young readers as they grow into caring, compassionate and loving individuals, who put kindness and inclusion above all. This is our contribution to the change we want to be and see in the world.

Our heartfelt thanks to Book Hub Publishing for their immediate and unwavering support for this project.

With Love For ALL,

Mary Helen, Max, Hugh and the Manatee

Hugh and the Manatee

The early morning rays of a late summer
sun peeked through the curtains of Hugh
Hanson's corner bedroom at No. 2 Violet
Hill Road. Hugh blinked at the light,
rubbed his bleary eyes and squeaked out
a loud yawn, just before his mother called

his name in a sing-song tone that was far too cheery for that hour of the day. He didn't mind, though, because she was announcing that his breakfast was ready.

It was Sunday morning. That meant a big, fat stack of pancakes slathered in whipped cream, topped with a smiley face made of the bluest blueberries, would be waiting for Hugh at the kitchen table. This was the last day of summer holidays before he would officially be in his final year at Druid Hills Elementary School. Hugh's mom had promised to take him swimming one last time at his favorite

place in the whole wide world;
Ballooga Springs State Park.

As always, Hugh made a grand entrance. He joined in as his mother sang their favorite "Good Morning" tune, before wrapping his arms around her waist, as he took her for a spin across the kitchen tiles. The well-worn black and white checkerboard pattern had doubled as a magnificent ballroom dance floor, for as long as he could remember.

He had just turned eleven in June and because Hugh and his mom lived on their own, his aunties and uncles liked to refer to him as 'the man of the house'. Hugh didn't really care for the title or the responsibility it suggested, and he would giggle nervously or find an excuse to leave the room whenever his relatives mentioned it.

After landing with a great big 'ker-plop' in his chair at the head of the table, *following an award-winning double twirl,* Hugh plucked a ripe, juicy, strawberry from a bowl of fruit on the table. He gently removed its green stem and leaves before carefully cutting it in half. Hugh then gave the blueberry smiley face a pair of ruby red lips before placing the leaves in the fluff of whipped cream that looked like a bushy hair-do. The fruit-face atop his pancakes was now smiling back at him, as if 'she' were incredibly proud of the new green bow in her hair.

When Hugh had mopped up the last drop of syrup with his final bite of pancake, he savoured the strawberry lips, which he had saved for last as a special treat. Hugh's mother had changed out of her night-gown and was now wearing a colorful, paisley patterned sarong. She ruffled his hair, kissed his cheek, and then wiped a spot of whipped cream from the tip of his nose. She told him to hurry and put on his swimsuit before the perfectly pleasant morning turned into a mid-day scorcher.

He didn't have to be told twice, because he loved going to the enchanted swimming hole at the state park. Since he had been a tiny tot of two or three, Hugh's mom had told him the most wonderful stories of the mystical creatures living just below the water's surface at Ballooga. She had convinced him that there were mermaids in that water and although he was now a very wise young man of eleven, he still got goose bumps when his mother spoke of the magic in these very special springs.

Hugh pulled out his favorite pair of swimming trunks from the bottom dresser drawer. He chose the tee-shirt his mother had recently given him for his birthday. Hugh had stared longingly at the pink sequined unicorn, hand-stitched on a bright lemon tee-shirt, matched with a pair of denim shorts on the mannequin with the pig tails in the shopping center window.

Even as a child, Hugh had always loved his style and the brighter the colors, the better. He looked around his room, adoring the way that his very favorite color had found its way into the check pattern in the curtains, the wispy clouds in the sunset printed on his bedspread and even a huge portion of the very stylish clothes in his wardrobe. It didn't matter if it was electric pink, blush, fuchsia or coral... the pinker the better, as far as he was concerned.

Hugh and the Manatee

Hugh admired his outfit in the full-length mirror at the top of the stairs then slipped on his Converse with the neon pink laces and headed out the door.

The drive to Ballooga Springs was always a treat. Hugh's mom would crank up the Broadway show tunes on the radio and they would sing beautiful harmonies at the top of their lungs. He especially loved when they arrived at the entrance to the springs.

The road back to the swimming hole was full of bumps, twists and turns. It was lined with the most beautiful Crepe Myrtles, whose perfectly pink petals floated gently on the breeze as if Mother Nature, herself, was scattering the blossoms to welcome them. The last big turn before the springs looked like a long, fluffy pink carpet.

Hugh asked his Mom to drive slower, so he could wave his hand at an imaginary audience of adoring fans. This was the spot where he always loved to pretend that he was pulling up in front of a brightly lit theater, in a big, fancy car to receive his latest singing and dancing awards.

When they had finally found a place to park, Hugh pecked his mother on the cheek, jumped out of the car and ran towards the crowd of swimmers splashing around in the shallow end of the water. It seemed the Hansons weren't the only ones who wanted to make the most of the last weekend before school started again.

With a novel she couldn't wait to finish tucked under her arm, Hugh's mom made her way to an empty wooden chair in the shade. She faced the springs and could see that Hugh was already at the water's edge, untying his flashy pink laces. She couldn't have missed him if she tried. His outfit was as loud and fabulous as his personality. She smiled to herself, so proud of the extremely unique and loving child she was raising.

Hugh found a place to sit on a jagged piece of concrete wall with a few steps that led down into the crystal-clear waters. He removed his shoes and dangled his feet over the edge of the top step.

Hugh admired his toes as they reflected in the water. He had painted the nails "Party Time Pink" the night before and he smiled at the way the flecks of glitter sparkled when he swished his feet around.

When he turned to wave at his mother, the sight that greeted him instead, made his stomach lurch. Lolly Lapowski and Cindy Snead, the two snippiest snoots in Druid Hills Elementary, were headed straight for him.

"Well, well, well, Cindy. Look who we have here! If it isn't sweet little *Hughlary Hanson*".

Lolly Lapowski had her hands on her hips as she made fun of Hugh. Cindy Snead, who copied everything that Lolly did, belly-laughed as she stood with her hands on her hips and sneered,

"Helloooo *Hughlary...*"

Lolly and Cindy had been teasing Hugh ever since they caught him playing with dolls from the *girls'* toy box in kindergarten. For six solid years they took every opportunity to taunt him, in and out of school. The town they lived in wasn't very big, so not only had he seen

17

the girls every day at school, but at every birthday party, every social outing and *every everything*, since the age of five.

Nowadays, their nasty little attitudes made him more annoyed than sad. Their cruel jokes no longer caused him to cry at night. He had grown past that. In fact, a year earlier, after yet another bullying incident, it was Lolly and Cindy's horrible words that had prompted Hugh to truly open up to his mother. He was nervous as he expressed his secret feelings about who he was inside. She had wiped away his tears, kissed his cheek and told him that there would only ever be **one** Hugh Hanson. She wanted him to love himself, embrace his awesomeness and live his life the way HE felt most comfortable. With a strong voice and her eyes moist with tears, she said,

"Don't ever spend a minute of your precious time trying to make other people feel more at ease with who you are. You are the perfectly perfect expression of Hugh. You are my bright spark...end of story".

He would never forget that moment.

Hugh had explained to his mom that he didn't like playing the same way the other boys did. He preferred to dress up in the pretty pink princess dress and glittery tiara from the costume box in his classroom, rather than kick a football or roll around in the dirt with the other boys. He *hated* to get dirty and always tried to keep his bouncy brown curls perfectly in place. His keen sense of fashion had been noticed by his peers *and* his teachers.

Hugh had lots of friends and had become quite popular with the girls in his class.

They liked the way he dressed and the very clever ideas he came up with at recess. He loved to get the girls to put on feather boas and silky scarves and put on shows for each other. They would sing and dance and he knew every word to every Disney musical ever made.

The boys, on the other hand, called him things like 'sissy' and 'princess' and, of course, Lolly Laposwki and Cindy Snead were the worst of the worst, screeching out "Hellooooo Hughlary", as they swished their hips and made kissy noises every time he was in their sight. The only boys who didn't torment him were the ones on his swim team.

Hugh was the strongest swimmer of them all, with his long arms and lanky legs. The school's Under 12's team had won a lot of competitions because of him. His team mates giggled *with* Hugh not *at* him, when he shot through the water like a long pink torpedo in his designer swim cap and very colorful swimsuit. They cheered wildly when he danced around the pool, blowing kisses to the crowd after winning yet another medal. He felt free in the water, away from judgement and where the other kids could see that he was **so much more** than their cruel comments suggested.

Hugh had now pulled his feet out of the water, attempting to hide his pink toenails from the girls. It was too late. Lolly let out an ear-piercing shriek, sounding like a cross between a hungry seagull and a wounded donkey. She nearly pulled Cindy's arm out of the socket as she drew her friend's attention to Hugh's pink pedicure.

Just as Cindy let out a squawk of hateful laughter, all three children gasped as very large pair of the bluest, round eyes began to surface in the water. Hugh sprang to his feet while Lolly shoved Cindy in front of her like a human shield. Great big bubbles were floating in the air and Cindy began to whimper in terror as the incredibly large head that was attached to the eyes now made its way fully above water.

"What *is* that thing?" Cindy cried, as Lolly continued to push her towards the 'monster'.

"I don't know", yelled Lolly, "but don't let it near me!" The two girls were wailing with fright.

"Shoo! Shoo! Get away, you filthy beast!" Lolly commanded the *thing* to leave.

25

Hugh, on the other hand, locked eyes with the great being, which he now recognized as the most unusual manatee he had ever seen.

It continued to rise out of the water like a steely submarine, until it was nearly eye to eye with Cindy and Lolly, who were not quite so confident and demanding anymore.

What sat before them, effortlessly floating half in and half out of the water, was hardly a monster. In fact, Hugh thought this mysterious creature might just be the most beautiful thing he'd ever seen. He could have sworn that it smiled and winked at him. It wasn't unusual to see manatees at the springs, but Hugh rubbed his eyes and shook his head to make sure he wasn't dreaming. This manatee was definitely smiling, and...it was *pink*.

Hugh's mom had given him picture books with facts about manatees (or *sea cows*) after he spotted his first one, when he was only six. He reckoned he probably knew more about the 'gentle giants' of the sea than most kids his age, but he had *never* seen a pink manatee in any of his books.

27

Lolly and Cindy remained paralyzed with fear while Hugh took a step closer. The manatee turned, nudging Hugh's leg affectionately. With one hand, he gently patted the head of the mystical sea cow. Everyone who swam at the springs knew that it was against the law to touch a member of this endangered species with two hands. Hugh had learned from a park ranger that it was only o.k. to touch a manatee at all, if they had touched you first. Hugh wondered if there was a special set of rules for *pink* manatees.

All of a sudden, the massive mammal began to hum. A pleasant, but peculiar sound seemed to come from deep inside as a bubble formed on its lips. Hugh was reminded of the giant soap bubbles he liked to create with his magic bubble wand at home. This bubble, however, was becoming much larger than any he had ever made and it shimmered ever so brightly with the colors of a rainbow.

The hum sounded like something Hugh had only recently heard. His mom's best friend had sent a care package of snacks, books and music from Australia for Hugh's birthday. There was one recording of an instrument that was unfamiliar to Hugh. It was native to the Australian Aboriginals and was a long, hollowed out piece of wood called a didgeridoo. As the hum became louder, Hugh was certain that's exactly what it sounded like...a didgeridoo.

The bubble continued to grow, as if 'in tune' somehow with the hum of the manatee. Within moments, it was so large that Hugh could have stood up inside of it. When it looked as if it couldn't get any bigger, the bubble softly broke away from the manatee's lips and floated towards Lolly and Cindy. For a few seconds, their screams could still be heard until it was as if the bubble had swallowed them whole. Hugh could see the girls pounding on the sides of the shimmery orb with tight fists and twisted faces. He could not, however, hear them scream any longer. The soundproof bubble had made them completely silent. If for no other reason, Hugh was grateful to the manatee for that.

With a deep breath, the melodic mammal carefully crafted a second mammoth bubble. When it was just big enough for Hugh to stand inside without bumping his head, the manatee gave a wink and gestured for Hugh to step in. He took a quick glimpse at Lolly and Cindy, who had stopped pounding and were now stomping their feet with temper, trying to burst their own bubble. Hugh giggled out loud as he stuck one leg in, followed by the other, straight through the rainbow sheen until he was standing right smack in the middle of its effervescence.

Hugh and the Manatee

It was surprisingly cool and refreshing inside and Hugh swore he could hear music. All at once, his bubble lifted into the air, followed by the bubble of a very shocked Lolly and Cindy. They hovered for a moment, just long enough for Hugh to catch a glimpse of the shady tree, where his mother sat reading her novel. If only she would look up, Hugh thought, Ms. Hanson would get the surprise of her life seeing not one, but three children suspended in thin air inside of rainbow orbs created by an enormous pink manatee! If Hugh hadn't been right there inside the bubble, he wouldn't have believed it himself! It seemed that some of the stories Hugh's mom had told him about the 'magical waters' at Ballooga Springs, *might not have been fairy tales after all.*

With an epic splash, the manatee dove into the still waters. The bubbles were sucked under water with such force, that Hugh squeezed his eyes shut and let out a yelp. It wasn't long before his mouth was hanging wide open, as he peeked out through squinted eyes at the beautiful sight before him. There he was, near the bottom of the springs, as if being pulled by an invisible rope behind this unusual aquatic creature. Right next to him, he could see two other mouths wide open, as the girls had stopped screaming and pounding and were now silent, in utter disbelief as they sailed beneath the surface of the cool, blue lagoon alongside Hugh.

It wasn't long before the girls discovered that they were still actually breathing. Their bubble was filled with clean, cool air. Lolly screwed up her nose, put a hand to her ear and asked Cindy if she could hear music. She could swear there was music coming from somewhere. The sounds made her feel tingly and...well...*good* inside. Whether she did or she didn't, Cindy immediately said that she heard it too, because there was *no way* Lolly was going to hear magical music without her.

The scene began to change quite dramatically and Hugh figured that the manatee was taking them out towards sea. The sun-filled waters of the shallow springs were now becoming a bit murky; deeper and dimmer. As if someone had just turned on the lights, a huge school of red-breasted and yellow-bellied sunfish surrounded the three bubbles. The curious fish reflected the fading light from the surface above and they glowed with magnificent shades of mandarin orange, canary yellow and ruby red, lighting up the grey waters around them.

Hugh couldn't help but exclaim out loud, yet speaking to no one in particular,

"Oh, they're beautiful! Just beautiful! Look at that luminous one over there!"

He pointed to a spectacular specimen that seemed to glisten as if painted with flecks of real gold. Its round belly was so orange it was nearly red and there were three distinct black stripes wrapped around its middle. Hugh smiled, as the fish reminded him of a photo he had seen of his mother as a teenager. She had been wearing a very cool wrap-around black belt over a neon orange top, way back in the late 1980's.

"She's just fabulous!" Lolly was absolutely mesmerized by the magnificent shimmer of the dazzling fish.

Quite unexpectedly, a soothing voice

began to speak inside all three bubbles.

"Yes, that *is* a very beautiful fish, Lolly. How interesting that you called **him**...*she*.

"Oh", said Lolly, looking all around her for the source of the voice. "It's just... I mean *he's* just so much fancier than the others. I thought..."

The music in Lolly and Cindy's bubble suddenly became a very distinct tone. The girls squirmed. They both felt something like warm honey pouring over the tops of their heads, oozing down to the tips of their toes, but nothing was there...it was only *a feeling*. As quickly as it had begun, the strange sound stopped and a quiet melody began to play again.

Hugh felt his bubble start to move. As they glided further out to sea, he noticed the most curious looking creatures scurrying along the sand. Darting in and out of bits of broken shell and seaweed, Hugh thought they looked very like the little spiders that he had seen hiding in the windowsills at his house.

Cindy, who wasn't a very big fan of eight-legged beings of any sort, screeched as she tugged at Lolly, pointing to the spindly legs of the spider-like creatures.

"Eeeeew!" She shivered with loathing.

"What *are* those *things* all over their legs? That's so gross!"

Hugh, a very big fan of the undersea world, spoke. Much to his surprise, not only could he hear the girls' voices inside of his bubble, apparently, they could hear him, as well. It was like being on an undersea speaker phone.

"I read about these in my aquatic biology book. They're called sea spiders. Those *things* you see on their legs are eggs. Those are baby sea spiders".

"Typical", replied a very irritable Lolly. "The moms are walking around with the babies hanging from their hips while the dads are free and easy. A woman's work is never done". She had heard her own mother say the same thing many times before.

Gently, the voice of the manatee spoke.

"How interesting that you assume that you are looking at a 'mother and baby' group, Lolly".

"Well, of course they are. *Hughlary* said

that those were babies attached to their legs. Mothers are the ones who have the babies and take care of them.

Duhhhh..."

Her tone was as sardonic as the pack of smirking sardines that had just swum past her bubble.

The tender voice of the manatee was kind as it carried on.

"It just so happens, Lolly, that while the female sea spiders lay the eggs, it is actually the males who carry and care for the babies until they are old enough to survive on their own".

Lolly and Cindy were flabbergasted. Once again, the music inside of their bubble was replaced with that curious tone, just before they felt the sensation of warm honey spilling over them again. A few moments later, the soft music returned. They looked at one another and wondered why they heard that sound *every time* the manatee spoke to them.

Hugh peered out dreamily at the fascinating undersea world he had only ever seen in picture books and on TV. He wondered if this was what it felt like when his goldfish, Shelly, looked out through her small glass bowl into his bedroom. It was all so enormous and colorful; a great big world with no end!

Hugh's daydream came to an abrupt halt as snorts of hysterical laughter filled his bubble. Lolly and Cindy were heckling a very docile looking creature, plodding ever so slowly along the ocean floor. Its shell looked a bit battered and there was even a spot of green algae growing on it because it moved so sluggishly. The girls thought it must be the *dumbest of the dumb* and immediately dubbed *him* "King of the Underwater Losers".

"Only a boy could move so slowly and be

so dull and ugly", they cackled heartily as they pointed, mocking the little brown blob.

It seemed that the girls' judgement and nastiness was air-tight and water-proof.

Without fail, that haunting tone filled the bubbles, the feeling of warm honey, followed by the caring, yet firm, voice of the manatee.

"Meet the ancient sea snail, ladies. These, as you say, 'ugly, dumb blobs', have managed to survive on Mother Earth for over five hundred and fifty million years. Not bad for a bunch of *losers*, don't you think? Not only does this species have the gift of incredible longevity, they are initially born male...and then, when they reach a certain size, they can change to female if there are too many other male snails around. The original *Trans Genders*, one might say. Because of their unique qualities, they have survived and thrived for millions and millions of years".

For the first time since leaving the shore of the springs, Lolly felt a slight tinge of an unfamiliar emotion. She was feeling...just a little bit...sorry.

Hugh marveled at the many different shades of color around him. Each fish seemed to glow with its own special blend of neon stripes, fluorescent tail fins and feathery plumes. A very interesting fish swam by, catching the attention of not only Hugh, but of the two girls.

"A-ha!" shouted Cindy. "That one is **definitely** a girl! She's wearing a full face of make-up".

No sooner than the words had come out

of her mouth, the quiet melody in her bubble changed to that odd, yet calming sound. The girls knew what was coming next; the feeling of warm honey and the 'feel-good' sensation from head to toe. They waited for the manatee to speak.

"How deceiving looks can be, Cindy. What you see before you is the Wrasse fish. While its face is, indeed, perfectly painted with an array of vibrant colors, this, in fact, is a male who *used to be* female. Traveling in groups that are led by a dominant male, if the leader dies of old age, disease, or is perhaps eaten by a lionfish or barracuda, the largest female of the group will actually grow new male organs and become the head of the school".

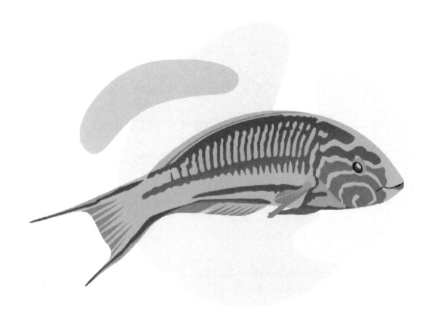

"Grow new male organs? That's repulsive!" Lolly had her very pinched, disapproving face on again.

"Repulsive?" The manatee chuckled. "I hardly think so. If it wasn't for the ability of the female to change, the Wrasse family of fish would have never survived their challenging environment over millions of years. Lucky for this species that the females never identified *who they were* or *the value of their role*, by *the body* they were born in to".

The girls looked over at Hugh, who had his

back to them but was motioning towards a cluster of powder blue and pastel pink coral. A most exquisite specimen paraded through the water. It magically became blue in front of the blue coral and as it shimmied towards the pink coral; its hue began to change to a blushing pink. Hugh recognized this fascinating dance immediately. He looked to his left and not too far away, a second horsey-faced fish swirled and weaved towards the first. He had watched a video on the internet of this mating ritual only a few months ago.

"What are they doing? He looks very

protective of something". Cindy had her face squished up against the bubble as Lolly looked over her shoulder.

"Don't be stupid!" Lolly replied, sarcastically. "That's a mommy and daddy seahorse. He might be protecting her, but I bet he's prancing around acting all proud, because she's just given birth to their babies".

"He's protecting the babies, alright" Hugh chuckled, as he continued to stare at the magnificent show.

Hugh and the Manatee

"Lolly, once again, you have judged the book by its cover. You are *partially* correct in your assumption." The manatee spoke with great patience.

"The male seahorse is, indeed, protecting their babies. Your error, however, is in presuming that the mommy seahorse gave birth to those babies".

Both Lolly and Cindy looked terribly confused. "But how else could...I mean the only way... boys **can't** have..." They were now totally perplexed.

The manatee took a deep, audible breath. The mystical tone was now, louder than ever.

"The world is a very diverse and interesting place, girls. Your understanding of what is 'normal' is limited to that which you have experienced so far in your young lives. I do not fault you for that. I do want you to understand though, that it is time for you to open your hearts and your minds to the idea that everyone and everything aren't exactly like you. Just because others look differently, act differently, love differently, live differently or dress according to their own unique styles, doesn't give you the right to bully or isolate them, *even if you don't like them or you disagree with their choices.*

There is room for all of the individual expressions of life on this earth. This is not a world of black and white, where only girls wear pink or boys play football; where only mothers and fathers raise their children together or those who are born into a certain type of body choose to live their entire life as that gender.

Above water, in your version of the world,

people, animals, reptiles and birds come from different countries, eat different foods and have many different colors of skin or feathers or fur. There are all sorts of fascinating rituals, celebrations and customs that may seem strange to some, yet are perfectly normal to others.

Take the peacock for instance; the females are brown, look washed out and very plain, while the males strut around with their enormous, fancy feathers, proudly showing off the most vibrant greens and iridescent shades of blue. There are countless examples throughout

61

the world that destroy the stereotype that girls should look one way and boys behave in another. That's what makes this such a special place.

Some children have a mother and father

like you, Lolly. Some, like Hugh, are raised only by their mothers. Others are brought up by a father or grandmother, like you, Cindy. There are pairs of mothers and unions of fathers who lovingly adopt children who would otherwise have no home. There are girls who love girls and boys who love boys, who decide not to bring any children in to the world at all.

There are girls and boys who love *both* girls and boys. There are boys who know in their hearts that they identify as girls and girls who know beyond a shadow of a doubt, that although their bodies might be female, they are actually boys. There are even those who don't really feel like either. They should be allowed to follow their dreams, explore the world through their own unique perspectives and live their lives in peace...and in safety.

You absolutely have the right not to agree, but you never, ever have the right to cause harm to others because you don't like their lifestyle or the way that they look. Lolly and Cindy, your words and your deeds have often caused harm to others. You are old enough now to take responsibility for your actions.

To love and be loved, to allow yourself to be open to all possibilities; to know that *everyone* is deserving of consideration and kindness...that is something wonderful to aim for in life".

Hugh felt his heart swell until it seemed as if it would actually burst. He sat, cross-legged in his bubble and he couldn't have stopped his tears even if he had wanted to. Lolly and Cindy stared at him from their bubble. They said nothing. In fact, he was certain that he saw tears glistening in Lolly's eyes. Cindy wasn't laughing. Her eyes were cast downward and she was anxiously wringing her hands.

Hugh suddenly became aware that the bubbles were on the move again. Much faster than before, they whizzed past schools of fish that blurred together in a kaleidoscope of colors. The music, the beautiful sound inside of the bubbles grew louder and more intense. Lolly and Cindy looked as if they were in a trance as they whipped past unusual formations of mottled rock and stringy seaweed, leaving a trail of sand clouds in their wake that shimmered like sparkly puffs of glitter.

A stream of light now entered the bubbles. Hugh was dizzy and it looked as if Lolly and Cindy were utterly dazed as they approached the surface of the water. With hardly a splash, the bubbles sprang up through the water and glistened in the light of the warm, late afternoon air. They softly glided towards a patch of sand under a great weeping willow tree. Children sloshed around in the shallow end of the springs as grown-ups looked on and smiled. No one seemed to see them. No one seemed to notice the enormous bubbles as they popped without a sound, depositing Hugh, Lolly and Cindy on their hands and knees, safely on shore.

Hugh shaded his eyes with his hand and looked out at the springs. Two enormous blue eyes peered out at him from inside a circular, rainbow ripple in the water. With a wink and a nod, the magical pink manatee submerged silently beneath the current, leaving nothing behind but a bit of sparkle and shine.

Lolly and Cindy began to stir, unsure of where they were or what had just happened. Lolly stared at Hugh with a mixture of fear and uncertainty. She reached down, grabbed a stupefied Cindy by the arm and the two girls ran towards the crowded park. Within moments, Hugh could no longer see them.

Unsure himself of what had just occurred, Hugh stood up, staggered slightly and set off to find his mother. With her novel spread open across her chest, she peacefully snoozed in the dying rays of sun, as afternoon slipped into evening. Hugh reached for her hand and his mother let out a little snort. She giggled and embraced him.

"Ooo! I must have dozed off, sweetheart. Is everything ok? Are you having fun?"

Hugh jumped into his mother's lap and gave her the most gigantic, squeezy hug he had ever given.

"Are you alright, dear heart? What was that for?" She knew that there was more to his embrace than he was letting on.

Hugh replied, his eyes brimming with

tears, "I just love you Mom and I'm so grateful that you have always loved me... just the way I am".

"Well, of course I do, my bright spark. There will only ever be **one** Hugh Hanson."

The Hansons packed up their things and headed for the car. Hugh's mom turned on the radio but quickly turned it off again. Hugh had fallen fast asleep before they had even made it through the twists and turns to the entrance of the park.

That night, Hugh barely ate any of his

dinner and excused himself to his room much earlier than usual. His mother thought he had simply gotten too much sun and was exhausted from a care-free day of swimming at the springs. Hugh laid out his clothes for school and packed his supplies in his new rainbow colored backpack with a furry purple pom-pom that hung from the zip. Before he climbed in to bed, he stared into the fishbowl on his desk. He carefully placed a few flakes of fish food into the bowl and watched as his goldfish, Shelly, gobbled them up. He wondered if she knew...

After a restless half an hour of feeling anxious about starting a new school year the following day, Hugh finally fell into a deep sleep. He dreamt of a wonderful underwater adventure, dancing seahorses, punk-rock Wrasse fish and... a pink manatee.

Bright and early the following morning, Hugh jumped out of bed before his mother even had the chance to call him. He quickly ate his breakfast, grabbed his backpack and kissed his mom goodbye.

"Have a wonderful day, my bright spark!" The Hansons lived just around the corner from Druid Hills Elementary School and Hugh had asked his mother if he could make the five-minute walk on his own this year. He was, after all, a sixth grader now. His mom had agreed, but she was just a little nervous as she stood at the door and watched as Hugh met a cheerful girl with long, silky braids at the end of their driveway.

"Hi, Ms. Hanson!" said Sally Sumner, the second strongest swimmer on the school's swim team, and Hugh's very best friend.

"Have fun, you two, and look after each other!" Ms. Hanson felt a wave of relief that Hugh wouldn't be heading in to school alone.

"We will!" shouted Sally, as she threw her arm around Hugh's shoulders and playfully pushed him up the street.

The school seemed much smaller than it had last year. Maybe it was because Hugh had grown a few inches over the summer or maybe, as it was his last year at Druid Hills, he was prepared to move on to bigger and better things. Sally gave Hugh a pat on the back and headed for her classroom.

Hugh took a deep breath and hoped that this year might be a little different than all the others.

Hugh had always enjoyed looking at the classroom doors on the first day of school. He liked to see the new and creative ways the teachers decorated to welcome the students back. Ms. Smith, the math teacher, had cut out multi-colored numbers and mathematical symbols and taped them all over her door.

Mr. Washington, who taught English, had photo-copied the covers of different books his students would be reading this year. He had colored them in and framed the entrance to his classroom. He had even turned his door in to a giant book cover entitled, "Eleven at Eleven", with a picture of a rather scruffy looking boy in mis-matched clothes and messy hair, holding a kooky looking clock that read 11:11. Hugh thought it looked rather interesting and he couldn't wait to see if it was on his reading list for the year.

Just as Hugh was about to check out the door of Mr. Talley's geography class, he felt a sharp jerk on his shoulder. He spun around to see his new backpack skidding down the hallway. Laughter erupted as

Connor Newsome went running towards Hugh's bag and began kicking it around like a soccer ball. Larry Lynch and Paul Pierson grabbed Hugh by the arms and stopped him dead in his tracks.

It seemed that Hugh wasn't the only one who had grown over the summer. Connor was much bigger than most of the kids (who had now gathered around to see what all the commotion was about). His fire-engine red hair was spiked up with greasy gel making him look even taller... and a bit scarier.

"Looky here, fellas. *Princess Hughlary* brought in a beautiful rainbow backpack today! I think my little sister has the same one."

Connor bellowed with fake laughter and gave the bag another kick as Hugh desperately tried to break free from the vice-like grips of Larry and Paul. The other children laughed nervously, afraid that Connor would start on them too, if they didn't.

"Awww, let *her* go", Connor mocked in a baby voice. "Come on *you big sissy*. Come get your backpack. No hard feelings, *sweety*."

Larry and Paul released Hugh so unexpectedly, that he went flying across the hallway and landed at Connor's feet.

Just as Hugh went to retrieve his bag, Connor kicked it again. Yet, this time, as it skidded across the floor, he saw a different pair of hands reach down and snatch it up.

"Oh, no," Hugh thought to himself. "This couldn't get any worse".

There, holding his bag, was none other than Lolly Lapowski. Knowing he was really in for it now, Hugh waited for the next stream of insults to come hurdling his way. What happened next left him thunderstruck.

He felt another pair of hands on his arm. He tried to squirm away until he looked back and realized that Cindy Snead was behind him, *helping him to his feet.*

Cindy brushed him off and then stomped over and stood next to Lolly. The two girls linked arms and made a barricade between Hugh and a now very angry Connor Newsome.

"Get out of the way, girls, this is man's business".

"Man's business?... Man? I don't see any men around here!" Lolly snapped back without a moment's hesitation. She, too, seemed to have grown a few inches and was glaring, eye to eye, at Connor.

"Do you see any men here, Cindy?" Lolly's dramatic look of fake confusion had now brought Connor into a full-boiled rage.

Cindy was now imitating his bitter and twisted face.

"Look everyone!" Connor jeered. "Little Hughlary has *her* girlie friends fighting *her* battles".

"We're not fighting anyone's battles, Connor. What you are doing...what you are saying...it's just wrong, that's all. It's just wrong! How dare you make fun of someone just because he likes different things than you?"

A few eyebrows were raised in the group that had assembled to watch the spectacle unfold. A couple of Lolly and

Cindy's past 'victims' could hardly believe what they were hearing.

"Yeah!" Cindy chimed in. "How would you like it if people made fun of you because of your red hair, Connor? Or what if they *accidentally* found out that my brother was at a sleepover at your house and *accidentally* found the fluffy little lamb that you **still** sleep with? Well? How would that make you feel?

Oops, Lolly! Did I say that out loud?"

It was too late... the other children had

begun to *baaaaaaahhhh* at Connor.

His face was puce and
it looked as if his
eyes might actually
pop out of their sockets.

"Stop it, everyone! Just stop it!" Lolly
was enraged.

"Now Cindy, that's not the way to do it
either. You apologise to Connor. Two
wrongs won't make this right."

Hugh could not believe his ears. Cindy

was aghast that Lolly had just turned on her, but not wanting to rock the boat with her bossy best friend, she gave in.

"Sorry, Connor," Cindy said reluctantly.

"This is a great big world Connor Newsome. There's room enough for everyone," Lolly fumed.

"Wait a minute! If this had been last year, you would have been the **first** one to call *Hughlary* names!" Connor protested.

"Well that was then and this is now. I've

changed and so should you. Everyone deserves a safe space, even you, Connor". Cindy stood next to Lolly with her arms folded and nodded furiously in agreement.

Just then, the bell rang. The children who had gathered, grabbed their things and scurried off to their classrooms. Connor, Larry and Paul were the first to take off running.

Lolly brushed off Hugh's backpack and handed it to him.

"I like your new bag, Hugh. It... umm... well... it matches your personality; colorful and umm... unique." She struggled for the right words as she attempted to let Hugh know that she really had seen the error of her ways.

"I like it, too", said Cindy. She gave Hugh an awkward pat on the back, and just like that, the girls picked up their things and headed to class.

"See you around, Hugh." Lolly called backed over her shoulder.

"Uh, ok, yeah... See you around".

Hugh stood alone. The hallway, which had been bustling only a few moments ago, was now silent. He could scarcely believe what had just taken place. Could it be? Could the same two girls who had tormented him for all of these years actually be the same two girls who had just protected him from another bully? Was it really and truly possible?

*Maybe this year **was** going to be different after all.*

When Hugh finished school that day, he ran home and asked his mom if she would take him back to Ballooga Springs.

"Really? You want to go back? We were only there yesterday, son. Sure, I can take you down there, but the swimming season is over for the year".

"I know, Mom. I just want to go for a walk by the water, if that's ok".

Hugh and his Mom had a great chat on the way to the springs. He even told her about what had happened in school that day. While she was concerned, Hugh's mom could tell that he had handled it very well, all by himself. She was shocked, but ever so grateful when she heard that the two snippiest snoots in Druid Hills had taken a stand for him.

When they arrived at the springs, Hugh said he would only be a few minutes and asked his mom to wait in the car. She reached into the glove compartment and pulled out her novel and told him to take his time. She loved when unexpected moments arose which allowed her to escape into her favorite pass time. Hugh could see a park ranger walking on the far side of the springs, but other than her, there was nobody else around. He walked to the waters' edge and sat down. He began to hum the same mystical tune that he had heard, only the day before, at that very spot.

Like a pot coming to a boil, the water in front of Hugh began to bubble and pop. Sparks of light flickered all around and it looked as if tiny fire flies were dancing across the water. There, just beneath a circular rainbow ripple, Hugh saw a familiar pair of eyes looking up at him, brilliant and sparkling, like two magnificent sapphires. Hugh slipped off his shoes and waded out until the water lapped against his knees. He looked down and smiled at the 'Party Time Pink' polish on his toes as the glitter caught the light and shimmered like tiny diamonds.

"I knew you would come!" Hugh could barely contain his excitement as the enormous pink figure rose half way out of the water to greet him. The manatee lowered its head and Hugh gently patted its rosy, wrinkled skin.

"I trust you had an interesting day, Hugh?" The manatee enquired with a curious expression.

Hugh had a feeling the manatee already knew the answer to that question.

"I... well... yes... you see..." Hugh wasn't quite sure how to say what he wanted to say. The manatee was quick to assist.

"I take it you would like to know why Lolly and Cindy had a change of...hmmm...shall we say...heart?"

"Yes! That's it! It all happened so fast. Yesterday they were simply awful and today, well... today they...

"They had a change of heart". The

manatee smiled with such kindness and wisdom.

"Yes. That's it! A change of heart. I'm so grateful, really I am, I just can't understand how..."

"How it happened so quickly?" The manatee finished Hugh's sentence. In his excitement, Hugh felt as if his words were getting all jumbled up as he tried to explain.

"Do you remember the beautiful music that all three of you could hear in your bubbles, yesterday?"

"Of course, I do", replied Hugh. "How could I ever forget?"

The haunting tune had played over and over in Hugh's head, ever since.

"Did you notice that each time I shared a new point of view for Lolly and Cindy to consider that..."

Hugh cut the manatee short. "The tone changed! Yes, the music would change to a specific sound *every time* you taught them a new lesson".

"Indeed", chuckled the manatee. "Well spotted, Hugh".

"Each time I introduced a new idea, rather than make the girls feel inferior, stupid or small, I reinforced this new knowledge with a tone...a frequency. And that simple, yet powerful vibration, Hugh, was the frequency of **love**".

Hugh let out a tiny gasp. He put his hands to his heart, feeling overwhelmed with emotion.

"You see, Hugh... anything is possible in the presence of love".

Hugh wiped the tears that were now trickling down his face. He had one last question to ask.

"There's one thing I don't understand. That music, the frequency of love; it was playing inside of my bubble, too. If Lolly and Cindy made such an enormous change, suddenly sticking up for the very person they used to hurt the most...what happened to me?"

The manatee appeared to glow with a magnificent, white light.

"You *allowed* them to change, Hugh. And that, my brave little friend, is the **power of love**".

About Dr. Mary Helen Hensley

Dr Mary Helen Hensley is an American-Irish Author, Healer and Motivational Speaker originally from Martinsville, Virginia and living in Athlone, Ireland for 22 years. She has published seven other books with Book Hub Publishing, including 'The Pocket Coach' and 'The Chakra Fairies'. Her memoir, 'Promised By Heaven', was published by Simon & Schuster in 2015 and she co-authored 'Bringing Death To Life' with Hachette Books Ireland in 2018, and 'Understanding is the New Healing' with Lisa Hagan Books in America and Book Hub Publishing in Ireland in 2019. She is currently writing a screenplay and working on the second book in her pre-teen gender identity series.

About Max Gordon

Max Gordon is an artist and graphic designer based in New York City. Originally from Virginia, he graduated from Wake Forest University with a B.A. in Studio Art. As a full-time graphic designer, he's worked mainly in branding and web design, but now Max has completed his first illustration project and has brought his aunt's story of Hugh and the Manatee to life. See more of his work on Instagram at @maxgordonart